A thin fire runs through me

Also by Kim Trainor

Ledi
Karotype

A thin fire runs through me

KIM TRAINOR

icehouse poetry
an imprint of Goose Lane Editions

Edited by Ross Leckie.
Cover and page design by Julie Scriver.
Cover illustration: *Rivers and Streams*, cyanotype by Krista McCurdy.
Printed in Canada by Coach House Printing.
10 9 8 7 6 5 4 3 2 1

Library and Archives Canada Cataloguing in Publication

Title: A thin fire runs through me / Kim Trainor.
Names: Trainor, Kim, 1970- author.
Description: Poems.
Identifiers: Canadiana 20220405360 | ISBN 9781773102252 (softcover)
Classification: LCC PS8639.R355 T55 2023 | DDC C811/.6—dc23

Goose Lane Editions acknowledges the generous support of the Government of Canada, the Canada Council for the Arts, and the Government of New Brunswick.

Goose Lane Editions is located on the unceded territory of the Wəlastəkwiyik whose ancestors along with the Mi'kmaq and Peskotomuhkati Nations signed Peace and Friendship Treaties with the British Crown in the 1700s.

Goose Lane Editions
500 Beaverbrook Court, Suite 330
Fredericton, New Brunswick
CANADA E3B 5X4
gooselane.com

Preface

A thin fire runs through me began involuntarily, as a way of writing my way through a difficult time; the title poem functioned as a response to heartbreak, followed by depression, and eventually, the progression of new love. I wrote steadily over a period of about nine months, from late summer 2016 through the spring of 2017, roughly one poem every two or three days, each poem a meditation on a different hexagram from the I Ching. The quotidian became interwoven with the political and the ecological. Through selection and juxtaposition of fragmented details, these hexagrams aimed to grapple with my own personal situation and to document the tenor of this time.

It is the run up to the election of Trump as president of the United States; Ratko Mladić is on trial at The Hague for genocide and crimes against humanity; there's the rise of populist fascism. The IPCC has not yet come out with its special report on 1.5 degrees of warming, but we're reading every day of the existential threat we face as the Holocene yields to the Anthropocene: sixty harvests left, wildfires, the losses to J pod — the endangered resident orcas who live in the Salish Sea. There's an opioid crisis in Vancouver's Downtown Eastside: every day comes news of more overdose deaths. Overseas, Syria is in the middle of a civil war whose cause, many have argued, is climate change, drought; every day comes news on the battle of Aleppo.

The quotidian offers us up minutiae — tweets, Instagrams, texts, social media posts, online news. We peer into other lives; we absorb words, headlines, violent events. We see and we don't see. These scraps are unintegrated, unintegrable, yet we carry them. At times, only poetry seems an adequate medium of response.

I. BLUEGRASS

My body is earth and blood and blue
I can't scour. I can't dig it out.

When I think I've lost you I collect words
to replace your body. Bluegrass. Dock Boggs. Banjo.

A handwritten sign in the window offers tattoos
and tarot card readings. Gather yarrow. Cast the I Ching.

I have been vigilant. *All night*
I was digging at your grave.

In morning sunlight your calm forms a skin,
a blessing on me.

*

Porteau Cove. Furry Creek. A train's whistle
threads Indian Arm in the dark.

I wake with the moon.
You have sent me a telegram.

The water is clay. Teal. Chalk. Bruised
pink as when petals rot.

I clothed my lover with petals and wounds
I need more words than you can give.

Spill of pine needles. The tide comes in.
The water does not taste of salt. Swallow it.

Crows burnt into your arms. One in flight.
One at rest. Pitch on your wrist and brow.

Yellow safety vest with orange stripes X'd on it,
hung up to dry on the bathroom door.

You come into me. *Fuck. I'm gonna come,*
you say. You come. You

come into me. The gulls too, the ships' horns
all night.

Hawthorn, whitethorn, thornapple, haw.
The bough groans and cries. Tie rags to it.

*

A banjo's notes plucked clean from the water. Sunday morning —
But I wanted to marry that boy from the mountains.

You tell me of railroad spikes and drone strings.
I offer Cherokee blues, Karen Dalton.

Consult the Book of Changes. I place it on your chest.
Methods: yarrow, three-coin, marbles, beads, or grains of rice.

Hexagram 23 — *bo*. Stripping. Splitting apart. Flaying.
The typewriter cracks letters open.

There is no way of telling. Write these words down:
She rings like silver and she shines like gold.

Signals intermittent on the island.
I make antennae with my body to receive your call.
Initials carved in the peeled green skin of the arbutus.
γλυκύπικρον, bittersweet's tattoo.

Is it Hexagram 2 — *kun* — field, reception, acquiescence, flow, or
39 — *jian*? Limping. Obstruction. Hobbled. Bound.

And when it comes, I can't read you.
The crows speak their own language.

Helicopter bugs whir out of the scorched grass at dusk.
Dark ideograms.

*

This morning it was Hexagram 62 — *xiao guo*. Small exceeding.
Preponderance of the small. Small surpassing.

*You couldn't squish me if you tried. You could lie
on an ant, and it would get up and carry you away to its lair.*

The size of a sperm cell is about 0.50 micrometres, or
0.002 inches. It cannot be seen with the naked eye.

Small things. The tip of a needle. A quark. A grain
of the universe. Too small for human instruments to measure.

All day you seep out of me.
As we lie together, the wind in the leaves sounds like rain.

How about Hexagram 18 — *gu*? Named for venom. Correcting.
Work on what has been spoiled. Decaying.

Overnight the Holocene yields to the Anthropocene. We leave
    signals
in the rock: radionuclides, plastics, carbon.

READ THE QURAN picked out in white on a rooftop.
The silver-skinned Fraser steps dripping from the mist.

You do not write to me.
I have been alone all day, all night.

We have smoked the earth.
Dig up any structure and you'll find chicken bones.

*

And when you are gone I embalm you
with words. Remove the tongue. Remove the eyes.

When they ask me about you, I say I've moved on.
There's this boy with an oud.

Always behind the barricades — no way in.
Your mouth a void.

So it was Hexagram 23 after all. Stripping. Flaying. Splitting apart.
The typewriter cracks letters open. Splintered words.

My face is riddled with holes.
All night I was digging at your grave.

II. THE BOOK OF CHANGES

36.

How is she become a desolation, a place for beasts to lie down in!
Each line a strip of skin torn from me.

Ming yi — darkening of the light. Brilliance injured. Intelligence
    hidden.
Hexagram 36, eclipsed.   ·

I meet a friend in a bar on Kingsway. We drink underground.
I'm getting pretty good at pretending I'm OK.

Run for the 97 B-line as the rain pours down.
Wet feet all day.

The black ink of my tattoo lies
under a sclera of dead cells. A claw

tears through the membrane. The breast. The wing.
Caw. Caw.

40.

This morning I decide on Hexagram 40 — *xie* — taking apart.
Deliverance. Untangled. Take everything apart.

Take a walk around Lake Lafarge.
Again. Again.

The crows are gathering.
Take the edge of the alphabet.

Take Venlafaxine. Take Zopiclone.
Some warm milk.

Begin the unravelling. The six-winged beings fly.
Serotonin and seraphim, all the orders of angels.

Holy, holy, holy. Touch my lips with coal from the altar.
I want. Purity. Light. Ardour.

( )

Is there a hexagram for glass? Clarity.
Seeing through.

Tempered. As molten glass hardens.
Its cutting edge.

A crow flies in through my window
and lands on my pillow.

Black coffee in a white cup. 14th and Main.
KEATS carved into my wrist.

The skies open.
Rain needles a ghost tattoo.

The Day of the Dead.
Wednesday morning.

12.

I wake every night in the small hours. One. Two. Three.
My blue flesh weeps.

Hexagram 12 — *pi*. Standstill. Stagnation.
Obstruction.

The man next to me in the café hums
tunelessly.

A poet sends me a text: `It's like I just keep falling
in on these beautiful worlds.`

I wake to Art Bell in the high desert. *Yaweh — God
Eternal within the body,* his guest insists, *coded CGAT.*

Words stick. Gangrene. Necrotic. 5-HTP.
MDMA. Violet.

29.

K'an. The abysmal water.
Plunging in.

The soul locked up within the body.
Light in the dark.

Christ wanders Main Street in sneakers and a laurel crown.
I have seen him before.

Votive candles on Cohen's doorstep.
God is alive! Magic is afoot. It is written in Montreal.

Do not look for him.
Do not look for him.

Water flows continually. It does not stop
until it fills every hole.

30.

Li. Radiance. Clarity. The clinging fire.
Light hath no tongue, but is all eye.

Gardeners wire trees at the lake's edge.
Screw in hundreds of glass buds.

A little girl in green antlers and sparkles barks
like a dog.

SPARE CHANGE PLEASE —
THANKS 4 YOUR HELP.

I read on the SkyTrain: Celan as a child drew burning
candles — *I loved its burning down.*

Fire has something within itself that perseveres.
Don't get me wrong. I'm not blue, just clear.

49.

Hexagram 49. *Ge.* Stripping away.
Radical change. Metamorphosis.

Commuters' screens shimmer like a sea serpent's blue scales.
Trump broods, *Saddam Hussein throws a little gas, everyone
    goes crazy.*

(Ten thousand Kurds.)
The world sheds its skin.

Chinatown. Venables. Clark. The Knight bus swerves,
skims twilight on Kingsway.

As a needle lays down fresh ink the blood wells,
is wiped clean. The letters feel like stitches.

Instructions for Care: Do not scratch or pick.
As it heals, the skin peels and shines.

52.

Fog off the inlet two nights running.
I crash on the darkened B-line.

Gen. Gn. Hexagram for the keeping still mountain.
Keeping still. Mountain.

This —
vowel so short as to be almost non-existent.

Thursday morning. Little Saigon. White girl with a tattooed thigh
waits for johns at the corner.

Against the din of Kingsway traffic, several cars
crawling past.

She stands perfectly still.
A word spills from her shoulder.

9.

Xiao chu. Hexagram for passive restraint.
Small harvest. The taming power of the small.

*Doesn't Pliny tell us that the centaurée cures torn
flesh?* Little blue cornflowers.

Boil this small flower with pieces of meat and
flesh assumes its living form.

Words are always remedies. The problems are large.
Violet. Cornflower. Haw.

I write this not to depress you but
to concentrate our minds on the scale of the task.

Pay attention.
We have only sixty harvests left.

32.

DOOM AT ALMIGHTY'S NEXT COMING.
And as the bicycle wheels passed — LIGHT.

In the Svalbard seed vault ten thousand seeds lie in metabolic stasis,
our wager with the future in their dark potential.

Pale radicles push through soil,
rooting for light.

Planet BINGO. **KAFKA's.** *Sunny Spot Café.*
Red neon beads on glass.

Open my notebook and write, *2 December 2016.* Scan the news:
EMERGENCY MEETING CONVENES ON ALEPPO'S "DESCENT INTO HELL."

32. Heng. Endurance. The long enduring.
Standing fast.

53.

＊

This is the hexagram for dialectical progression.
Jian. Infiltrating. Step by step.

There have been six rains of one hundred thousand poems.
La Moneda. Dubrovnik. Guernica. Warsaw. Berlin. London.

(The avant-garde of mad bindweed bearing cups
from which trickled a blue drunkenness.)

A man in a yurt tells me his plans to etch two million words
on a 2" × 2" nickel plate, to blast into space. But I forget

to send him a poem. Another man
injects his codons into an unwitting bacterium. *Poetry*

is the cockroach of the arts. Tardigrades in their tun state
have survived on the moon.

2.

Kun. The receptive earth.
Field, flow.

Broken lines.
Yin.

How can we enter the poetisphere of our time?
An era of imagination has just begun.

This guy playing his red guitar outside the Noodlebox.
Broadway and Main: the Tattoo Junction.

There are words for: Naked. Making.
Bittersweet. Poetry. Inked on skin.

And then I found this girl (very crazy of course)
(like me I guess) who talked language.

45.

Ts'ui. Gathering together. Grass root effort.
Contraction. Stitching. Network.

The code is a learned mechanism that historically sutures
the organic body to symbolic language.

Two strong lines bring about
the gather together.

Hoods drawn against the wind, which snatches
cigarette smoke, words from our mouths.

I'm trying not to unravel. I stitch one line
to the next, one letter after another.

The machinery of the signifiers composing themselves on the typewriter,
impressing themselves unto paper — is not entirely in her control.

20.

The ablution is complete, the sacrifice not yet made.
Light retreats so the dark can rise.

Rocky the caretaker died the other day. His mattress and box spring
propped by the dumpster.

Ratko Mladić is on trial at The Hague: there is witness:
people staring at you from the earth: their eyelashes, lips,
    fingerprints.

At the Krajina Identification Project, a "bone window"
is extracted with precision blades. I look through.

Remains are meticulously washed, and
a biological profile established. I look away.

Genetic fingerprints are slipped into digital files.
20 — *Kuan. Ritual washing of hands.*

21.

Shi ke. Hexagram for biting through.
To tear, to gnaw. Let justice be administered. Let judgment fall.

The words of Mladić are transcribed —
Let's drive them out of their minds so they cannot sleep.

And who will die today of fentanyl?
And who by law?

Inject the burning shot,
euphoria rushing. And then the dark.

Ears unfurl in the fields.
Eyes bloom from the soil.

The single bullet holes through the skulls
of these men from Hozica Kamen are articulate.

60.

Jie. Articulating.
The joints that divide

a bamboo stalk. Spine.
Tongue.

Touch the edges of words —
Radical talk. Glottal. Stop.

*Archilocus' written texts break pieces of passing sound
off.* Ar-tic-u-late.

Mismatched spoons from the Sally Ann.
Racks of winter coats I flick through

a motley syntax.
I. You.

19.

A shoeless woman rides the 7 down Powell tonight.
Socks in shreds, bares her breast, sings, *it's heavy metal*

not heavy mental. It's a metal. This is where I get off.
This bus. Off. To the warehouse.

Metro News ladies in gauzy, blue-and-green fairy wings.
I take a copy — a new injection site has been approved.

Implicated in the concurrent process of the erotogenic
inscription of a symbolic body over the organic body.

Anticipate the winter solstice,
light.

I wait for my bus at Hastings and Main.
Thinking Hexagram 19. *Lin*. Approach. Advance.

24.

Fu. Returning. The turning point.
St. Lucy's Day. The year's midnight.

The judgment: To and fro goes the way. On the seventh day
comes return. It furthers one to have somewhere to go.

Boxcars inked CHINA SHIPPING along the curved tracks
by the East Van docks. Turquoise rock salt in moonlight.

I slip on the ice. Scrape my knee.
Cut my wrist.

We drink wine, argue Tibetan prayer wheels
and the nature-culture divide.

Poem as imbrication, *an overlapping of successive layers of tissue*
in the surgical closure of a wound.

33.

Dun. Retreat. *The power of the dark is ascending. The light
withdraws. Hostile forces in formation.*

I wait under the marquee for you. Our second date. Cohen's name in lights.
I swipe through posts: *15 December 2016 —* OPERATION TO EVACUATE

REBEL-HELD ENCLAVE IN ALEPPO NOW UNDERWAY
A line of green buses, no end in sight.

No slight challenge, but the stakes are very high: literally,
survival of organized human activity in any direct form.

You'll say, *It's the Unetaneh Tokef — Who by sword and who by beast?
Who will be safe and who will be torn?*

As you stand next to me. In the red light of the Fox
there's a tower of song.

22.

Cobalt glow of screens as we queue for the bus.
Ban Ki-moon trending on Twitter:

Aleppo is now a synonym for hell.
They are playing roulette with #fentanyl.

Liquid crystals leak blue into faces.
This lady in a sweater of sparkling gold eyes.

In this line, I want to include an angel.
Angels. *Chayot Ha Kodesh. Ophanim. Erelim. Hashmallim.*

Seraphim. Malakhim. Elohim. Bene Elohim. Cherubim. Ishim.
Beauty in fire blazing up.

We settle in for the long ride.
22 — *Bi.* Grace.

56.

Hexagram 56. The mountain stands still, fire above.
Wildfire. Travelling stranger. *Lu.*

A voice pierces the white noise.
I cup my ear —

@Mr_Alhamdo: *To justify our elimination, even your governments will say we are terrorists. Don't believe them and be angry for our blood.*

@Mr_Alhamdo: *I will make a periscope telling you exactly what happened.*

One zettabyte of data in a gram of DNA.
How many words leak out if you cut a vein?

Our third meeting you say, *If you ask too much of me I'll run.*

57.

Yun. Slow penetration. Submission. The eldest daughter.
Wind sifts

the roots of growing
wood.

Frost crystals knit blackberry thorn. I stumble,
you reach for my arm.

Sword fern is slick with ice. You feed me
a Chinese pear. I straddle your thigh.

It snows all night. You text me:
Angels are welcomed in.

You tell me licorice fern grows on maples.
Taste this sweet root.

27.

Here's the hexagram for swallowing — 27, *Yi*. The firm
lines of the lips. Wide-open mouth.

I buy a Bic in the colours of the Habs. Flick it
with my thumb — blue sparks, fire.

The waters above are summoned
by the waters below.

God comes forth
in the sign of the Arousing.

Snowberries and camas root.
Thimbleberry. Fir tips.

Now. I open my mouth for you now.
Teach me to forage. Snow bramble. Wild ginger.

31.

Hexagram 31. *Xian.* Conjoining.
Tension. Union.

The male is placed below the female — his repression
is her desire.

We walk across sheets of snow,
are lost for hours in your bed.

I am reading fragments of Sappho. 74A...*goatherd*...*roses*...
74C...*sweat*...

A thin fire runs through me.
More pale than grass.

78...*not*...*longing*...*suddenly*...
...*longing*...*blossom*...

44.

Kou. Coupling.
Suture. Stitch by stich.

The principle of darkness obtrudes again.
The maiden is powerful.

In the dark you sing niggunim,
join intellect to heart, branch to tree.

You go down
on me.

I write a line, then
cross out half the words.

There is less and less
More, more.

48.

This hexagram taps into aquifer and
voice resounds.

Jing. Water drawn from a well,
through a plant's fibres, out of earth.

Your exegesis on Genesis, eco-midrash
on the second law of thermodynamics. *Let there be light.*

Orca J34 is towed to land near Sechelt.
There are toxins in Puget Sound.

There is darkness
upon the face of the deep.

Yehi'or. Let me translate you
out of the original tongues.

55.

Are you hungry? I have a pomegranate in my bag.
Your mouth on my breast.

A pomegranate! *No. A grapefruit.*
Your mouth on my mouth.

You give me the seven fruits of Israel — pomegranate,
fig, grape, wheat, barley, olive, honey.

Be not sad.
Be like the sun at midday.

Be like the seed around which flesh grows.
Quicken and green.

55 — *Feng.* Abundance.
Movement of flame.

14.

The fire in heaven above shines far, and all things stand out in the light and become manifest.

Ta yu. The small feminine possessing
largeness. Tenderness.

I let you
see me.

Cultivate seeds that store the energy of stars.
Shine adamant, like the sun.

Slender roots suffuse clay.
Ta yu. Ta yu.

Hekla. Fengdu. The gates of horn.
How many ways into the deep.

58.

It snows all day and the city shuts down.
My fingers root in your hips.

Tell me about Ora and the Judean hills at dusk.
My lips graft to your thigh.

Tell me about Dharamshala.
The deodar cedars leafing with prayer flags.

In Sydney fireworks bloom in the dark.
Temple gongs strike the new year.

Pale hyphal tips tender the soil.
My eyes seed in your veins.

58 — *Tui*. Open. The joyous.
Two bodies of water conjoin.

64.

We ji. Not yet fording. Move warily,
like an old fox crossing ice.

I have not seen you in five days. When we meet
you tell me of all the creatures born at dusk, between worlds.

The frogs who are disappearing.
Their translucent skin.

Created at twilight on the eve of the Sabbath,
these defective creatures who cleave neither above nor below.

The mouth of the swallowing earth, mouth of Miriam's well,
mouth of the ass. The Shamir worm.

Where no form exists, all forms are possible,
all is open. Spirits. Ghosts. Ophanim.

46.

Sheng. Ascending. Sprouting from the earth.
Hexagram for pushing upward.

In four ways is man like an animal, in four ways like an angel.
A man eats, shits, fucks, and dies like an animal.

We walk through Block F on Musqueam ground.
Cutthroat Creek slips into culvert.

Here is lichen. Lignin rot. A wren.
Mycelia entwined.

Tamped snow.
The scorched husk of a cedar.

You fuck me. We are one being
with wings and myriad eyes.

59.

Huan. Dispersing. Dissolution.
No remorse. He is crossing the sea.

The forest has scattered its seed on snow. Green dangling
catkins of alder like a page out of *Women in Love.*

Writing secures the word against phonemic dissolution,
just as eroticization secures an articulate body.

The body is diagrammed by the lover.
...red little spikey stigmas of the female flower...

You say, *Flowers, not buds, male,*
not female catkins. Katteken. Little cat.

You correct me.
I articulate you.

8.

Bi. Holding together. *Water fills up all the empty places on the earth and clings fast to it.*

You are reading about soil: *the enmeshment of particles by sticky networks of roots and fungal hyphae.*

You are reading the Zohar: *As this alphabetic flow proceeds, it is gradually transposed into* yod, mem, he,

which spell yammah, *meaning sea.*
In Kabbalah, each letter is a path to wisdom.

I am learning to spell again.
Read me from right to left. Use your mouth.

Teach me the alephbet.
Use honey.

3.

This hexagram has *explicit sexual content.*
A blade of grass splits soil.

Zhun. Sprouting. *Difficulties arise from the very profusion*
of all that is struggling to attain form.

Words rot. *Consonants which act directly on the body,*
penetrating and bruising it.

My tongue. My throat, canted.
Your hips torque.

Seminal roots
probing with tips.

Rigidity of stalk that can pierce concrete.
Tenderness.

51.

Zhen. Hexagram for the arousing thunder. Symbol
of startling movement. Thunderclap.

Clang! of a cymbal.
Absorbing vibrations.

Coarse letters soften in a foreign tongue —
zayin, lezayen, kus.

Cunt slashed in the page.
/k/ hardened to "fuck."

The single letter is a condensed cipher of other meanings,
itself a miniature inner discourse.

Inscribe me.
Be explicit.

29.

It turns and returns. This hexagram for impasse. *Jian.*
Limping. Obstruction. Bound.

You have sown much and harvested little, you eat
but never have enough, drink but never have your fill.

I passed by you and saw you weltering in your blood.
A single phrase and I am undone.

This morning you are everywhere
I am not today. A faintly heard nigun.

Holding fast the heart swelling.
I drink but never have my fill.

I stumble through simple words, even
my name I must relearn — *kuf, yod, mem.* Struck dumb.

5.

Hey, I'm jumping in the shower. The door is open
if you come before I'm out. Come in.

I subject your texts to an exegesis
worthy of Rashi scouring the Talmud.

More intense concentration on the words and their relations,
including even the physical shape of the letters and even the text's
punctuation.

I wash thy blood from thee.
I anoint thee with oil.

I gird thee about with fine linen.
I cover thee with silk.

5 — *Xu*. Waiting. Moistened. Biding one's time.
Crossing the great river.

26.

Da chu. Taming power of the great. Surging headwaters restrained
by a dam. A cooking pot with its lid. An egg. A seed.

Late January. Each morning the news is bleak.
PRESIDENT WON'T RULE OUT TORTURE AS A WAY TO

"FIGHT FIRE WITH FIRE."
I text you a slender filament of words.

Each morning, Quan Yin sealed under glass.
O goddess, have mercy.

And something about light.
Put the stars back in the sky.

Take the glints out of the netherworld.
We must fight fire with fire.

35.

Jin. Advance of consciousness, forwardness,
getting the idea, *comes the dawn.*

Come dawn I am walking north towards Broadway.
A coyote crosses four lanes of traffic.

Quan Yin, have mercy, have mercy.
Skinny and feral. Slantwise. Loping.

The dawn comes, just as God poured light into vessels.
On their shattering, the divine leaked into the world.

I gather up these seeds of light.
I sift every text you send.

Multiplicity of creation.
Coyote crossing white lines.

13.

Line one reads, *The beloved is at the gate — no harm!*
(The door's unlocked-come in!)

Tong ren. Fire rises to heaven.
This hexagram is a union of forces,

gathers beloved friends and lovers, gathers
the ancient sunlight of trees, as I

come to you this night. Gather me
as you would tinder or

blackberries in the forest.
Kindle me.

A musky sweetness slipped
under the tongue.

50.

Ting. The cooking pot. Feed the people.
Hold and transform things in the vessel.

At the student co-op they serve borscht in a chipped bowl.
Someone's talking Hegel in the corner: "It's amazing to see desire

become a metaphysical concept." But I want. *De sidere.*
And the four beasts had each of them six wings about him

and they were full of eyes within, and they rested not day nor night,
    saying,
Holy, holy, holy.

Longing resides in the body.
Hips, chest, wings, eyes.

Ting — The judgment: you are the sacrificial vessel.
Take what you find to hand and transform utterly.

28.

A friend texts me the headline: IT MAY ONLY TAKE 3.5% OF THE
POPULATION
TO TOPPLE A DICTATOR WITH CIVIL RESISTANCE. With you

I am transformed. *Ta kuo.* The ridgepole bends. Adjustment.
Great exceeding. Critical mass.

It was done with Pinochet in Chile.
Milošević in Serbia.

But this: *although it looks wonderful that people are demonstrating,*
it's actually rather frightening, because it's generating a crisis
situation —

The northern flicker's long call, *kyeeeeeer,* like a warning.
Its rapid drumming on metal pole.

You draw me close. We sleep.
Through the snow-tamped night.

43.

We talk for hours and then come
long silences. I retreat. You

hold yourself apart. The snow falls. My body
is lost for millennia in the ice.

You travel a great distance
across the steppe, pour cupfuls

of hot water. Use a small hammer. My scapula
chiselled out. My wing

spread under your fingers,
the scapulae pulled taut.

Kuai. Displacement. Parting.
Breakthrough.

6.

You open my body
from collar to sternum

and down, in a T
to the pubis.

There is more blood
than you expected.

Ribs cracked and breastplate lifted out
so you can see my lungs and heart in situ.

Then you sew me back together
with crude stitches.

Sung. Conflict. Quarrelling.
No joy without sorrow.

4.

Red shoots along the Fraser. Green water and snow.
Red twig dogwood? Willow?

You finger the slender wood, look for dried leaves or buds.
You long for expertise.

There are simplicities you don't know. I teach you
how to lift the bowl of miso soup to your lips,

how it fills you like spring light, like the estuary's
salt water. Let it fill you up.

Man is capable of being in uncertainties.
Let us live with this.

Take my hand. Let's walk again
by the meandering river.

11.

You send me O'Keeffe's *Flower of Life*, black-lipped
petals clasped in white:

I want to climb inside the black
and pull the white cowl over my head.

I send you her *Lawrence Tree*: *I love this one.*
How you can see the stars through the branches.

Like standing at Camosun bog on a dark, clear night.
I've never been. *I'll take you.*

Calyx of sepals.
Pull me down over your eyes.

T'ai. Holy marriage.
Conjunction. Peace.

47.

The first line reads, *She enters a dark valley.*
Another day of *sweet-and-sour reality.*

The headline reads, **100,000 NATIONAL GUARD TROOPS TO ROUND UP UNAUTHORIZED IMMIGRANTS: AN UNPRECEDENTED MILITARIZATION.**

Kun. Hexagram for oppression. Repression,
confinement. Entangled. Dried up.

The oppressiveness of doubt exhausts
our inner resources.

There is sour. Troops gather at the border.
The proto-fascist scenario.

There is sweet. Salmonberry on your tongue.
Camas lily. Mulberry. Wild ginger.

61.

Zhong fu. Inner truth. Sweet restriction.
Centre returning.

The body is washed and immersed in the ritual bath.
Wrapped in a white linen shroud. Placed in a box of pine.

The shape of the poem is a self-enclosing spire
which darkens its source.

You text me from the trailhead, below the treeline.
You will traverse the Garibaldi Névé.

When you are gone I read only blue books
with numbered scholia.

Bury me under a cherry tree —
remember I am the one who asked you this.

54.

Kuei mei. The girl gives herself in marriage. All voluntary
  relationships
between human beings require care.

If we permit ourselves to drift along, we come together
and are parted again as the day may determine.

You are in the mountains. When you are gone
there is no trace of you.

I open my notebook and write: When you are gone
I read only blue books with numbered scholia.

9.3 The person in the poem is always being-for-another-altogether.
The person in the poem has no sake.

I come looking for you.
You read me in the morning light.

41.

I take the kitchen scissors and cut my hair.
Take the razor. Scrape my neck.

Scrub turquoise polish off my nails.
Strip clothes.

Sun. Diminishing.
Strip yourself bare.

Eviscerate
the pages.

Blue worms.
Cut lines. Nerves.

Drain blood.
Cut it all away.

10.

Let thine eyes look right on, and let
thine eyelids look straight before thee.

Lu counsels cautious advance.
Don't get bitten. Watch your step.

You fuck me and wings crack my spine.
Does poetry work this way?

Ophan. All seeing. I put my mouth on you.
Eyes open on the inside of your thighs.

Black slash of each letter
on the virgin page.

You cover your face to shield me.
Seraph. Burning one.

17.

Sui. Following. *Masculine rigidity moves*
below the tender feminine.

You fuck me and a window opens.
I am clear as tempered glass.

In aperture, the self is characterized as identical or
"flowing with" the world.

This blue appears like the sea and the sea
appears like the sky and the sky appears

like a god
walking down a blue road.

You point to a tree outside my window
and call it sweetgum.

1.

Qian. Hexagram for the green fuse.
Force. Strong action. The key. The god.

Mechanism by which Eros swoops upon an unsuspecting lover
to wrest control... wings are an instrument of damage.

Take me into the clearing to hear the laughing ravens.
Quork, quoork.

Use your fingers to unpick me.
Your lips to drink from me.

The next station is Inlet Centre.
Tracks darken in rain.

Kiss me with the kisses of your tongue.
Tell me about *tzimtzum*, infinite light.

III. SONG OF SONGS

37. *Jian Ren* — Fire and Ground

Behold, thou art fair, my love.
As a mountain goat. A lily.

My beloved is unto me as a cluster of cumphire
in the vineyards of En gedi.

As the scales of the western red cedar
on swordfern trail.

As the blue of the lupine grown from seed
that flowers only in the second year.

Behold, thou art fair, my love.
Our bed is green with licorice fern.

Our house is cedar
and our rafters, amabilis fir.

15. *Qian* — Yielding

My beloved knocks, saying, *Open to me.*
I open to my beloved.

I am blackberry and bluegrass.
Ragwort and sundew.

Sphagnum. Bog laurel.
Cedar and fescue.

As the little blue-black berries
on salal's pink stem.

As the licorice fern, its rhizomes
anchored to maple.

You are the bittersweet,
its berries split red in the sun.

53. *Jian* — Slow Progression

In the clefts, in the knots, in the smooth
grain of the old growth.

In the small pink tongues of the corydalis
and the green bracts of the lilac.

Something grows from a blueprint.
A seed. Incremental.

In the cone and the catkin.
In the flakes of lichen.

As the apple tree among the trees of the wood, my beloved.
Feed me with dust, I sit in your shade.

For lo, the winter is past,
the rain is over and gone.

7. *Shi* — The Army, Multitudes

Who is the one who looks forward? He is terrible as sunlight,
shining as an army with banners.

I go down into the garden to see the green spikes
of Solomon's seal.

You text me the Russian for black soil, *chernozem*.
You pierce me with green tips of iris.

Turn your eyes away from me, for you
have overcome me.

Your shield of western red cedar.
Your sword on your thigh.

Or ever I was aware, my soul made me
like the chariots of Amminadib. The burning of seraphim.

38. *Kui* — Estrangement

By night on my bed I seek you whom I love
and I find you not.

I will arise and look for you
in the empty streets of Cedar Cottage.

I will seek you in the broad ways,
in the narrow alleys.

I will ask the watchman —
see you him whom my soul loveth?

Tonight I look for you
but I find you not.

There is no place
I will not go.

16. *Yu* — Providing For

Who comes out of the wilderness like woodsmoke,
like the drift of rain?

The streams are rising.
The salmon return.

Look for me in blue spruce and cloudberry.
Witch hazel, violet.

Madrone and juniper.
Licorice fern. Cherry.

Awake, north wind, and come,
come south.

Let my beloved come into his garden
and eat his pleasant fruits.

34. *Di zhuang* — Great Invigorating

Come, my beloved, let us go forth this morning —
let us go into the muddy lanes.

Let us get up early and see the yellow forsythia.
The white magnolia.

Let us go to the bog to look for sundews.
For thimbleberry and the blossoms of Labrador tea.

I am sphagnum and chernozem.
The waters of Musqueam Creek.

Your hips are like lillies, your legs as cedar saplings.
You are most lovely. Your mouth as sweet as Nootka rose.

Let us go into the damp streets.
There I will give you my love.

25. *Wu wang* — Fidelity

Press me as a seal on your heart.
Carve your name on my arm.

I seek him whom my soul loves.
I hold him and I do not let him go.

The coals thereof are coals of fire,
this vehement flame.

Water cannot quench love.
Floods cannot drown it.

Love is strong as death.
Cruel as the grave.

I reach for you in the night.
But you are gone.

42. *Yi* — Augmenting

Stay me with flagons, comfort me with apples.
I am sick with love.

I charge you, O my sisters, by the swordfern and Oregon moss:
Do not stir, do not awaken my love.

You are in the mycelia and subalpine trails.
You are in the yellow cedar.

You are in the eye of the wind,
in the dark-eyed junco and the flicker's call.

Until winter comes, I lie in your shade.
Black plums everywhere stain the ground.

Until the day breaks and the shadows flee, turn,
my beloved. *Be like a young hart on the mountains of Bether.*

63. *Ji ji* — Already Fording

You have clipped my breath.
You have staunched my tongue.

Swordfern. Sphagnum and cedar.
Spikenard, fescue.

Your lips
a braid of scarlet.

Ani l'dodi v'dodi li.
Your voice a *nigun.*

Coals of fire touched to lip,
held too long.

Come with me. Arise my love
and come.

Notes

I. Bluegrass

Song lyrics (in italics) are drawn from renditions of Appalachian folk songs by Ola Belle Reed.

II. The Book of Changes

The I Ching, or Book of Changes, is a book of ancient divination whose origins can be traced back two and a half millennia. It has been described as a "philosophic taxonomy of the universe" and consists of sixty-four hexagrams, each offering a cryptic reading. These sixty-four hexagrams are all built from eight trigrams, which are said to have been created by Fu Xi "in order to become thoroughly conversant with the virtues inherent in the numinous and the bright and to classify the myriad things" (Richard John Lynn's translation of the Da Zhuan, or "Great Commentary," *The Classic of Changes: A New Translation of the I Ching as Interpreted by Wang Bi*). Later commentaries and interpretations have accrued.

This section offers a sequence constructed from each of the sixty-four hexagrams of the I Ching. A hexagram is composed of six stacked horizontal lines, consisting of either yin (broken line) or yang (unbroken line). By means of yarrow stalks or coins, one of the sixty-four hexagrams is cast, and its description used as guidance in a dilemma or query the seeker has posed. Often a hexagram will have changing lines, one's present hexagram leading into a future hexagram. Change is the only constant in life.

Throughout, quotations in italics, with the exception of those noted specifically below, have been drawn, in roughly this order, from the following sources: Gaston Bachelard, *The Poetics of Reverie: Childhood, Language, and the Cosmos*; Mutlu Konuk Blasing, *Lyric Poetry: The Pain and the Pleasure of Words*; Anne Carson, *Eros the Bittersweet*; Allen Grossman, "Summa Lyrica: A Primer of the Commonplaces in Speculative Poetics," in *The Sighted Singer: Two Works on Poetry for Readers and Writers*; Susan A. Handelman, *The Slayers of Moses: The Emergence of Rabbinic Interpretation in Modern Literary Theory*; and the King James Version of the Song of Solomon. References to the I Ching come primarily from the James DeKorne website (https://jamesdekorne.com/GBCh/GBCh. htm), as well as from IChing123.org, deoxy.org/IChing, and Richard Wilhelm's *I Ching or The Book of Changes.*

Hexagram 49. *Hussein throws a little gas.* A comment made by Trump at a December 2015 rally in Tennessee. These words were revisited during the fall 2016 election campaign.

Hexagram 53. *Six rains of 100,000 poems.* Refers to a peace campaign in which poem leaflets were dropped over six cities that had previously experienced bombing campaigns targeting civilians.

Hexagram 9. *I write this not to depress you* and *We have only 60 harvests left.* George Monbiot, "The 13 Impossible Crises that Humanity Now Faces," *Guardian,* 25 November 2016.

Hexagram 32. *Emergency Meeting Convenes on Aleppo's "Descent into Hell."* CNN headline, 30 November 2016, as approximately thirty thousand civilians fled in the wake of government advances in the Syrian civil war. The UN has since argued that this evacuation, overseen by the ICRC, was complicit with the Syrian government and constituted a war crime.

Hexagram 20. The trial of Ratko Mladić for crimes of genocide and crimes against humanity ran from 2011 through 2017. Italicized quotations in 20 and 21 are from an article on the Krajina Identification Project, which used forensic techniques, including DNA sequencing, to identify victims of the Bosnian War, twenty-five years after its end. Ed Vulliamy, "Bringing Up the Bodies in Bosnia," *Guardian,* 6 December 2016.

Hexagram 33. *No slight challenge.* Interview with Noam Chomsky on the rise of fascism and the existential threat of climate change. Paul Mattick, "The Stakes Are High: An Interview with Noam Chomsky," *The Brooklyn Rail,* December 2016–January 2017, https://brooklynrail .org/2016/12/field-notes/the-stakes-are-high.

Hexagram 22. In 2016 in British Columbia there were 922 overdose deaths due to drugs laced with fentanyl and carfentanyl ("B.C. Overdose Deaths Now Surpass 2016 Total, Coroner Says," CBC News, 12 October 2017). Many of these deaths occurred in the Downtown Eastside, and were reported upon almost daily in 2016.

Hexagram 56. @Mr_Alhamdo. The Twitter handle of Abdulkafi al-Hamdo, a citizen-journalist from Aleppo who documented the ongoing battle for his city via tweets and embedded Periscopes.

Hexagram 48. Orca J34, an eighteen-year-old male of the endangered southern resident J pod, was found dead near Sechelt on the Sunshine Coast on 20 December 2016. The shíshálh Nation has now taken possession of J34's skeleton and renamed him *kwentens ʔe tesinkwu*, "guardian of the sea" ("Orca Skeleton Goes on Display," CoastReporter.net, 11 April 2019). *Yehi'or*: "let there be light."

Hexagram 26. *President Won't Rule Out Torture.* "Trump Won't Rule Out Torture As a Way to 'Fight Fire with Fire,'" CBC News, 26 January 2017.

Hexagram 28. *It may only take 3.5% of the population.* Erica Chenoweth, "It May Only Take 3.5% of the Population to Topple a Dictator — with Civil Resistance," *Guardian*, 1 February 2017.

Hexagram 47. *100,000 National Guard Troops.* "Donald Trump Considered Using National Guard to Round Up Immigrants, Memo Suggests," *Guardian*, 17 February 2017.

Hexagram 10. *Ophan*: singular of *ophanim*, a class of celestial being, often identified as angels. The myriad-eyed "wheels" of Ezekiel's vision.

Hexagram 1. Kabbalistic reference: the *Ein Sof*, "Infinite Light," withdraws himself from the world to create a conceptual space for other beings to emerge.

Acknowledgements

My sincere thanks to:

The editors where some of these poems originally appeared. "Bluegrass" won honourable mention in the *Fiddlehead*'s 2017 Gustafson Prize and appeared in the spring 2017 issue. Early versions of hexagrams 30, 49, 52, 9, and 32 appeared in *CV2*. Hexagrams 57, 27, and 31 were published in *Qwerty*; 60 appeared in the *Literary Review of Canada*; and "Sweetgum" (43, 11, 47, 61, 54, 10, 17) was longlisted for the 2018 CBC Poetry Prize.

Jennifer Zilm, who falls into beautiful worlds.

Ross Leckie, my brilliant, tenacious editor. His early-morning, long-distance phone calls were a master class in poetry.

Julie Scriver for her beautiful cover design, Martin James Ainsley for hawk-eyed copy-editing, and everyone for their care in the making of this book at icehouse poetry/Goose Lane Editions.

These poems were written in the late summer and fall of 2016 and through the winter and spring of 2017, on the traditional, ancestral, and unceded territories of the Snuneymuxw, xʷməθkʷəy̓əm, Skwxwú7mesh, Səl̓ílwətaɬ, and kʷikʷəƛ̓əm Nations.

Kim Trainor is the author of the poetry collections *A thin fire runs through me*; *Karotype*, described by Don McKay as "a crucial text in the work of reimaging what it is to be human;" and *Ledi*, a finalist for the Raymond Souster Award. Her poems have won the Fiddlehead's Ralph Gustafson Prize, the Malahat Review Long Poem Prize, and the Great Blue Heron Prize. Her poetry has appeared in the *Best Canadian Poetry* and Montreal Poetry Prize anthologies, as well as many journals, including *Dark Mountain* and *Anthropocenes (AHIP)*.

Trainor has collaborated with the musician Hazel Fairbairn on a series of films based on her book *Ledi* and worked with composer Yi Ning to produce an art song of her poem "Blackmud." Together with artist Amy-Claire Huestis, Trainor has curated "walk quietly / ts'ekw'unshun kws qututhun," a guided walk at Hwlhits'um (Canoe Pass) in Delta, BC, that features contributions from artists, scientists, and Hwlitsum and Cowichan knowledge holders. Trainor lives in Vancouver, the unceded homelands of the xʷməθkʷəy̓əm, Skwxwú7mesh, and Səl̓ílwətaɬ.